Lu and Billy

by Pauline Cartwright
illustrated by Rob Mancini

SCHOOL PUBLISHERS

Requests for permission to make copies of any part of the work should be addressed to School Permissions and Copyrights, Harcourt, Inc., 6277 Sea Harbor Drive, Orlando, Florida 32887–6777. Fax: 407-345-2418.

HARCOURT and the Harcourt Logo are trademarks of Harcourt, Inc., registered in the United States of America and/or other jurisdictions.

Printed in China

ISBN 10: 0-15-350636-9
ISBN 13: 978-0-15-350636-9

Ordering Options
ISBN 10: 0-15-350599-0 (Grade 2 On-Level Collection)
ISBN 13: 978-0-15-350599-7 (Grade 2 On-Level Collection)
ISBN 10: 0-15-357809-2 (package of 5)
ISBN 13: 978-0-15-357809-0 (package of 5)

11 12 13 14 15   0940   15 14 13 12 11 10

Lucy wanted a bird for her birthday.
The whole family went to the pet shop.
"There must be a hundred birds
here!" said Thomas, her little brother.

It seemed like that to Lucy, too. She looked at each bird carefully.

"I want a different kind of bird than all of these," she said.

Finally, Lucy found the one she wanted. It was a cute little parakeet with green feathers and small bright eyes.

During the ride home, Lucy decided that her bird's name would be Billy.

Lucy told Dad, "I chose a parakeet because parakeets can learn to talk. I'm going to teach him!"

"You'll have to be patient," smiled Dad, "it will take Billy a while to learn."

Lucy cleaned Billy's cage. She made sure he always had water and seed.

Every day she would say to her parakeet, "My name is Billy."

6

Lucy's brother Thomas would
also say, "My name is Billy."

"Don't do that!" Lucy said. "I'm
teaching Billy to talk."

7

In a short while, Billy learned to perch on Lucy's finger.

Lucy would pet Billy and say to him over and over, "My name is Billy."

8

"My name is Billy," Thomas repeated.
"Don't do that!" Lucy told him.

When Billy had become very tame,
Lucy sometimes let him out of his cage.

"My name is Billy," she called as he
flew by.

"My name is Billy," called Thomas, too.

"Don't do that!" Lucy told him angrily.

One day, Lucy was busy doing her homework. Thomas ran in and said, "Lucy, come quick! Billy just talked." Both children raced to Billy's cage.

Lucy was so excited she could hardly talk herself!

"Billy, talk to me," she said. Then she waited for Billy to talk.

Billy looked at Lucy with his bright eyes. His beak hardly moved, but Lucy heard him talk.

"Don't do that!" Billy said.

Lucy couldn't believe her ears.

14

Think Critically

1. Why did Lucy choose Billy instead of the other birds at the pet shop?

2. What caused Billy to say *Don't do that!* at the end of the book?

3. How do you think Lucy felt when she heard Billy talk?

4. What things did Lucy do to care for Billy?

5. Do you think a bird makes a good pet? Why or why not?

 **Social Studies**

Write a Paragraph Lucy got Billy from a pet store. Write a paragraph to tell about why customers (buyers) might want to buy a pet and why the pet store owner (the seller) might be selling pets.

School-Home Connection Tell a family member about the story. Talk about the things we can teach some pets to do.

Word Count: 317